PGGC – PEESHAUN'S GUY-GIRL CODE

HOW TO GET OVER YOUR EX

Atewo Laolu-Ogunniyi

How To Get Over Your Ex

PGGC – PEESHAUN'S GUY-GIRL CODE

A PGGC Book by Atewo Laolu-Ogunniyi
@skukipeeshaun

Book Design & Published by:
Emphaloz Publishing House
www.emphaloz.com
07038259005

To Omolere

TABLE OF CONTENTS

CHAPTER 1

FIRST OF ALL, INTRODUCTION

(They have served you breakfast)

Break ups aren't always meant for make ups.
Sometimes relationships end
in order for you to wake up.
- Anonymous

So, they have served you breakfast... lol.

Okay I'm not laughing, before you get upset at me now ***straightens face*.**

It's just that they have served me breakfast too in the past, in fact I've been served premium breakfast like 3 times in my life.

I remember a girl that broke my heart when I was in Uni. She left me and followed a man that drives a BMW ***I'm cry***

She had long moved on, but me I was still there nursing heartbreak as if I was the first man on earth to fall in love. One random day, months after we had broken up, I decided to send her a poetic text to showcase the condition of my heart to her.

See the text I sent, word for word below:

Baby, when we parted you took a part of me with you. A part of me that I cherish so much, a part of me that I can never get to share with anyone else. That part of me was you.

She replied:

Okay.

You see we look back at the crazy things we do when we're in love and wonder

"Was I mad?"

For the non-Nigerians reading this book, 'Being served breakfast' is a term that people in Nigeria use to describe someone going through a heartbreak.

So for instance if I get my heartbroken in a relationship, my friends would say "Oh sorry, you have been served breakfast"

The term is used in a comical way, in an attempt to lighten the mood of the person going through the heartbreak and to let him/her see that everybody goes through these things. You are not alone.

That being said, WELCOME!

This book is going to seem less like a book and more like a conversation between you and I. My intention is that by the time you're done reading this piece, your mind would have shifted to a different frequency that would make your moving-on phase as easy as possible.

When our relationship comes to an end, but we're still in love with our ex, the heartbreak can fling us through any of these different stages

Denial, anger, bargaining, depression, acceptance.

We all go through heartbreaks differently; I've seen people jump from denial straight to 'acceptance'

I've seen people get to 'acceptance' but they didn't really move on because they remained angry for years, as they felt betrayed by their ex.

Whatever stage you're in, we're going to arrive at true acceptance by the time you're done with this book. Not only that, you're going to have the mindset that would get you ready for the awesome future that is coming your way.

I know right now some questions are bugging your mind:

Was the break up my fault?

Would I find another person like him/her again?

When would I find someone that we'll understand each other this much?

Women, who most times are heavily emotionally invested in a relationship, might start pondering on how she wants to start this long-emotional-journey all over again with a new guy, getting to know him to the point that she can allow herself to be this emotionally vulnerable again.

What if the next guy is even worse than my ex?

Did I over do things? My friends always told me about this my bad attitude, damn! Now see where it has landed me.

One moment you're feeling like the whole entire break up is your fault, the next minute you're angry, convincing yourself that your partner could have been more understanding and could have sacrificed just a little more.

The last but not the least of these haunting thoughts is thinking that your ex is going to find someone much better than you.

What if this babe finds a guy that loves her for the woman she is, a guy that never complains about her nagging or being too possessive?

Or...

He always said I have too much drama, what if he finds a girl that can tolerate all the things I couldn't, and love him without trying to change him?

Over-thinking and over-worrying always set in when a person is going through a heartbreak and that's where most of these thoughts are coming from

CHAPTER 2

SHOULD I UNFOLLOW MY EX?

(Yes! Make that U-turn for now!)

When you're stalking
your ex's pic on social media
and you mistakenly like a pic from 2 years ago.
Now you gotta deactivate your account
and start a new life in China.
- ***Anonymous***

This was supposed to be chapter 7 of this book, but after reading through, I decided I'll bring it to Chapter 2, so we can discuss it quick and get it out of the way

Life is a game of energy. Everything in the universe is energy, both the visible like cars, houses and the invisible like electricity, air, **human emotions** etc.

Tony Robbins says the strongest force on earth is the human emotions, and I agree with him. That is why my focus throughout every page in this book is directed at getting YOUR EMOTIONAL ENERGY to the right place.

Anything or anyone that dampens your energy would hinder you from tapping into your full potential. Sadly, I know some people who have been stuck in a cycle of energy draining relationships for too long.

So I get this question from a lot of people who are going through a heartbreak moment. They're wondering if they should unfollow their ex on different social media platforms (and that includes WhatsApp)

I'm always shocked when people say, 'It would look immature'...

Excuse me? Immature?

The truth is, social media has become a very invasive part of our lives and if you don't control what you view on those platforms, you can end up having an awkward day with the images you see on there.

You need to understand that unfollowing your ex does not mean you're enemies, or that you're fighting them.

Your ex doesn't even have to be a bad person, maybe you guys still share a vibe and you still check up on each other once in a while, but the truth is, there's no way that seeing status updates from him/her would not send your mind into thinking-mode... it will! Every time you bring out your phone and you see his or her status icon highlighted, the wave of curiosity would take over you and next thing, you're clicking and consuming the very content that would make your moving on process harder.

Back to the people who think "Oh, it would look immature". We are talking about your mental space here. Since when did it become immature for someone to protect their sanity? Your mind can be very vulnerable during a break-up phase, you'll overthink things, you'll turn to FBI, analysing every picture, every location on your ex's pictures e.g *He's at the beach, but he doesn't like going to the beach. Who took this picture for him?*

Then you'll go on to the social media page of the girl that you suspect he was talking to, and start searching if she posted any pictures at the beach lately. Burning unnecessary amounts of mental energy and draining yourself.

Or if you're a guy, you check your ex's status update and you see that she's having a girl's night out, you start stalking all the girls in her video, checking their own pages to see the whole event from all possible angles. *"Why is she hanging out with these girls, she knows these group of girls are negative influence, I need to call her and advise her, so people don't start thinking she's like these girls"*

Oga! Calm down, don't call anything o. You are your own headache now, you are your own priority now. So unfollow, make that U-turn, you get it, make that YOU-TURN, your focus has to be on you now.

You might still not agree with me on this idea of 'unfollowing your ex'.

You see it's not so much about the act of 'unfollowing', it's more about unplugging yourself from that energy you shared with your ex, as it's not serving you anymore, and if you still hang around it, if you don't create mental space in your mind, you're not going to be able to move on and welcome your 'next'.

The right and perfect person can walk up right up to you, and you wouldn't notice them, simply because your energy and vibe is still stuck in your past relationship. So if you don't want to unfollow, then use the MUTE button, this allows you to stop seeing a person's updates on your timeline. The reason I put this as chapter 1 is because, one of the most important things to do both in and out of a relationship, is to protect your energy. It is deeply important that you master little ways you can protect your mental space.

CHAPTER 3

SHOULD I STAY OR SHOULD I LEAVE?

(Uncertainty)

I'm not telling you
it's going to be easy,
I am telling you
it is going to be worth it
- ***Art Williams***

Before I advice anyone to walk out of a relationship, I first of all point out to them that a working relationship is not always 'positive vibes' all the time. Many people that we admire as 'couple-goals' are usually very forgiving and understanding of each other's shortcomings, a lot of sacrifices go into those relationships that we look up to.

So, it's can be an error to leave a relationship at the first sign of discomfort.

But then, the effort to make things work cannot be one-sided. You cannot carry the emotional burden of your relationship alone. You can bend, adjust and inconvenience yourself here and there, but if your partner is taking all your emotional investments for granted, then it gets to a point where you have to re-evaluate and think of yourself. You should not remain with a person whose actions has started to encroach on your self-esteem.

If a person is treating you like you're not even there, always cancelling plans on you, to the point where your self-confidence has started to drop, then you have some hard decisions to make.

So what happens if you're currently at that point where you're asking yourself *Should I stay or should I go?*

A relationship is most draining, when it is at the edge of a break up, especially when you have poured your heart into the relationship, and this is a relationship you had high hopes for.

The advises that you would be getting at this point can also be very confusing. Some friends would be telling you to forget the relationship and not look back e.g "You deserve better, you're a Queen.

If you're a guy, your friends could be telling you "Forget about this girl, she's not worth it"

At the same time some other friends would be telling you to still try to hold on and try to make it work, maybe by forgiving your ex for what he/she did or by begging them to come back, depending on the situation of your break up.

The final decision lies with you. You have to look at the situation from a very honest angle. I know it's not easy, but sometimes, that decision that's not easy, turns out to be the best decision we can make for our sanity.

If the scenarios below describe your situation, then my advice would be that you should leave that relationship:

1. If the arguments you're having are not just basic arguments caused by personality differences, but rather you argue because the other person continues to do things they know are deal-breakers for you.

2. If you have lost your voice in the relationship, such that anytime you try to speak on the way your partner is hurting you, he/she makes it seem like you are complaining unnecessary. You are the one being stressed, but then they make it seem like they are the one being stressed.

3. If your partner is cheating and continues to do so directly to your face not caring how you feel. (Some people don't mind staying with a cheating partner, so this point applies to people who can't stand 'cheating') Of course, you can forgive a cheating partner, if they're remorseful, I know marriages where cheating was forgiven either by the man or the woman. But if you're with a partner who consistently cheats to your face, not giving a damn how if affects you, then I would not advice that you remain with such person.

4. If your partner's family don't like you, and you can clearly see that your partner is not going to prioritize you over their family. This can be very dangerous down the line, especially if the relationship goes on to become a marriage.

5. *It's okay to play the fool, but it is not okay to become a fool in the process.* If you have decided to let a lot of things slide, for the sake of peace, and you have been doing this for a few months, expecting that your partner would realize that you only did that for the sake of stability, but then they start to act like those things you tolerated should become the new normal.

6. Domestic violence must be a deal breaker for you! If he/she has been physically violent in the relationship before, that's a huge red flag. And if it has happened a second time, then you shouldn't even hang around to wait and see if it would happen a third time, please just leave!

Read the 6 points above well, and be very frank with yourself. There is a place for sacrifices and hanging on, and there is also a time when you have to grab the bull by the horns and make that decision to walk away.

Most times this feeling of uncertainty is even more stressful than the act of breaking-up itself, as you don't know where to concentrate your energy, should I focus on hanging on, or should I start focusing on healing.

Another thing that makes people unsure of leaving is fear-of-the-unknown future. And when you're walking out of a relationship, you just don't know what to expect next in your love life.

What if the next person I date is even worse than this?

CHAPTER 4

WILL I FIND ANOTHER PERSON TO LOVE AGAIN?

(Capital Y.E.S)

If you're brave enough
to say goodbye,
life will reward you
with a new hello
Paulo Coelho

I personally feel this is one of the most important chapters in this book, so let's first begin with some **real-life stories** before we dive into the advises I have for you.

I know a lady who stays in America, she's Nigerian. Let's call her Bunmi (*names have been changed)

Bunmi was dating a Nigerian guy, who managed to find his way to the US. They were very close and everyone knew them together. Eventually, with her help, Bunmi's boyfriend got settled in America and got a high paying job in the tech world. Months down the line he started changing, his perspective of life had shifted and he began feeling like Bunmi wasn't the type of woman he would want to settle with.

There were red flags which Bunmi had seen earlier on, but as she was eager to have a man and settle down, she swept most of the warning under the carpet. To cut the long story short, he frustrated her so much in the relationship, with cheating, violence etc. that they had to break up shortly after their 2nd year anniversary. She had invested a lot of time and emotions into getting him to have a better life with her in America, and here she was, coming up short and empty handed.

She felt as if the world would end and went through different phases of anger, resentment, self-pity and **FEAR**

Fear, that very ingredient that makes a lot of people remain in a relationship that they should be bouncing off from. Let's examine some of these fears

Fear of what people would say- *Screw people and their opinions, most people don't even know what they're doing with their own lives, so who are they do tell you how to live yours*

Fear of being alone- *The hardest time to be alone is the immediate moment after a break up, but honestly it is not as horrible as your mind is making you think it is. Yes, there will be nights of tears and heartaches, and that's very normal because you really did care about this person, but at the end of this sharp-sudden-pain is a better version of you. The period of hurting is supposed to be short, but if not handled well, a person can go on hurting for months or even years. In the coming chapters, we would talk about how you would ride through this period.*

Fear of not finding another person to love again- *This fear never plays out. It never ever plays out. I have seen this happen many times without number, you will always find another person to love again. Always!*

And it was this 'fear of not finding another person to love again' that gripped Bunmi. She actually considered agreeing to ridiculous conditions that the guy was bringing forth e.g. cheating, domestic violence. Eventually she received some sense and let the relationship go. That was singularly the wisest decision she ever made.

She went through 6-8 months of healing, and eventually, an older guy who she used to crush on started checking up on her. He had learned of her break up through a mutual friend. This would have been the last person she would imagine would pop up in her life. He asked her out a few months later and they soon got engaged. Not only is he older and calmer, he is more understanding, a full family man. He doesn't even stress her at all. He just looks at her like a baby sister when she's having her girly mood swings. And oh, I don't know if this is an extra point, but her new man happened to be way richer than her previous guy.

This is not some Disney romantic movie o, this is real life.

Don't ever doubt the fact that you shall find someone to love, you will even find someone better.

If you are doubtful of the story, I just told you, then let me tell you about my own elder sister. She got married at 33 years old, thirty freaking three, do you know how desperate a woman can be at that age? The guy she was dating broke up with her when she turned 30, he was controlling and abusive, but she kept thinking she could fix him. When they broke up, she literary gave up on the idea of ever getting married. Lo and behold, some dude that she did NYSC with saw her, and they started talking. They got married 2 and a half years later, they have been married for 9 years, I have not heard them argue once. He is the type of husband who comes home from work and cooks for his wife, he looks after their babies as much as she does. She couldn't have had it any better.

I know the two examples I gave above are women, but a lot of men go through similar situations.

I know a guy who didn't want to leave his badly behaved girlfriend, just because she was popular and beautiful. I explained to him that she might be the girl you want, but is she really the woman you need? Fear of not finding a woman who was as pretty and popular made him stay and condone a lot of nonsense. After months of sacrificing his self-confidence and feeling useless as a man, he let the relationship go. I told him he needs to re-evaluate what he looks for in a woman. His ego seemed to be dictating too much of his choices in women. He took my advice and in his words, he said it suddenly seemed like he had gotten extra eyes. He started seeing a lot of beautiful women who weren't a slave to vanity. Not only did he find a better woman, she was even more of his spec than the other lady who he wasn't compatible with.

Now, before we go thinking that we are perfect people and the other person is always the wrong one, let me point out that when two people break up, sometimes it's just straight incompatibility and no one is really at fault.

Sometimes our 'ex' is not even the bad person, sometimes it's us. Maybe there is something in your character that you need to work on and your ex is the lesson that life has been trying to teach you. The thing about life is that, we shall be taught the same lesson over and over again, until we learn it.

Honest self-assessment is necessary after separation from a lover and self-assessment can be a hard thing to do.

Naturally we are good lawyers for our own mistakes, but quick judges for others people's errors.

If you are part of the problem, if you have drama in your blood, then that drama part of you is gonna follow you into your next relationship, unless you work on it. Sometimes we need to take some time off dating to work on ourselves.

Of course, the next person you would date, might be able to tolerate your dramatic side more, or they might not be able to stand it as much as your ex did. Whatever the case is, it is best you look in the mirror and identify what excesses you might have, that is if you have any. Compare some traits that your siblings, friends or colleagues might have tried drawing your attention to, and decide to work on it.

As much as I want you to analyse some of the personal traits you might need to work on, I don't want you to overly blame yourself if **loving your ex too much** was one of those traits.

The act of loving is good, it was the element of doing it too much that wasn't healthy.

If you love someone too much, is it coming from a place of need or dependency?

If it stems from a place of need, you will be selfish and you won't know, if it's coming from a place of excess-emotional-dependence, you will choke your partner and you would think they are the one wronging you in the process.

Love is supposed to be selfless, but when you are loving your partner only the way it feels good to you, then you have reversed the whole idea of love as your selfish interest has sneaked into the picture. So now you're thinking "but I'm only expressing how much I love him/her". Little did you know that the trait you're giving off at that point is selfishness, the werey just dey disguise as love ni.

Of course, there's a difference between asking for basic attention and choking a person, I don't want us to mix it up.

A man I was coaching a while ago, told me he was okay going 3-4 days without talking to his fiance, as they were in a long-distance relationship and it got on his nerves when they had to check up on each other every day or every 2 days. I told him that, talking daily to someone you have already engaged is not too much at all. The conversations don't have to be long all the time, but just touch base with one another. He made some adjustments so he and his lady could meet each other halfway and he realized it wasn't so bad after all. So in their own case, it wasn't a matter of the lady asking for too much, it was the guy who wasn't used to sharing himself with another person and a healthy relationship requires sharing a piece of you with your other half.

Loving someone too much from a place of dependency, can make us allow unimaginable nonsense. For some reason, we become attached to the idea that we can only be happy through this person's presence, when this happens, you would let them walk over you till they no longer see value in you. So in this case you're not choking the other person, you're choking yourself. Surviving on the little doses of love they give you, while you lose your true self in the process.

Now back to answering the question we are asking in this chapter.

Yes you would find another person to love again, don't allow your mind to play tricks on you. Don't start looking around at all the people that are currently asking you out and saying to yourself "There's no husband material among these guys" or "There are no good girls out there anymore etc.

You're trying to use your present circumstances to predict the future- NO! Don't do that!

When the right person comes, it would be in a way and manner that you least expect. You just play your part, simply *become the lover that your dream lover deserves* and he or she would inevitably show up.

I know we use the word 'FIND' when we talk about 'finding love' but in reality, you don't find true love, you attract it. You don't find the perfect person, you attract him/her. And that is exactly what's going to happen to you right now.

YOU ARE GOING TO ATTRACT THE RIGHT PERSON FOR YOU!!!!

CHAPTER 5

MINDSET

(Less Memories, More Imaginations)

Once your mindset changes,
Everything on the outside
will change along with it
-Steve Maraboli

Right after a break up, the person who was most hurt from the separation tends to live a lot in the memory of the just-ended relationship. The silly thing our mind starts to do is that we apportion more blame to ourselves than we deserve.

"Oh maybe I shouldn't have shouted"

"Maybe I should just have accepted his aggressive behavior like that"

"Maybe I should have allowed her to nag as much as she wants, it's just her nature".

I'm not saying you are a saint, but I know that if the relationship ended against your wish, you would start to look for reasons why the break up was your fault.

Even if, to some extent it was your fault, there is a huge chance your mind would guilt-trip you more than necessary.

We also start to reminisce on the relationship as if it was better than it actually was. You'll start telling yourself "It really wasn't that bad, at least I was still happy every now and then".

Stop it! It was that bad!

Same relationship that drained you and made you cry endlessly? C'mon don't let your mind play these tricks on you in hindsight.

Everything still ties into the fact that you didn't want the relationship to end, you have gotten so used to what you shared with your ex and now that things have to change, it's hard to make that change and search for something new.

This why the word 'Comfort Zone' exists.

Now, being in your comfort zone doesn't necessarily mean that you are comfortable in that zone, it just means you are in a familiar zone.

This is why you would see a person in a relationship or marriage that is killing them slowly, and they would just not be able to walk away.

It's not because they're comfortable or happy where they are, it's because they're familiar with that situation, and they would rather stay in a familiar zone than take a chance at something better.

It's your subconscious mind at play here and your subconscious mind doesn't like change. Once we get into a relationship, a lifestyle or a routine, our subconscious mind locks it into our reality as what we call HABITS and it becomes part of who we are at that present moment.

I'll repeat it again, YOUR SUBCONSCIOUS MIND DOES NOT LIKE CHANGE, IT LIKES THE FAMILIAR.

This is why you need to become conscious of how your mind works at this point. 90% of the bad feelings you're getting is from your thoughts running wild and I want you to know you have more control over the situation than you realize.

Right now, the battle of moving on is between you and you. Your brain knows you need to stop thinking of this person, but your subconscious is not cooperating.

When one of my guys was going through a break up, he stopped watching his ex's social media stories, stopped checking her WhatsApp status and all. He successfully did this for 2 weeks, but one day he had a relapse, he just couldn't hold it anymore. He went ahead and binged-watched all her activities on social media for hours on hours. When he was done watching it all, he was emotionally drained. What did he gain? He gained 1000 unnecessary questions added to his already worried mind. It's not only women that go through these emotional hits, a lot of grown men go through it also. Love and desire are the two strongest of human emotions and anyone can be a victim of their power.

So don't be like my friend, you have to CONSCIOUSLY stop your mindset from wandering to where it shouldn't. That's why in the title of this chapter, I said *'less memories, more imaginations'*

In your mind, travel into a future-loving-relationship, let your thoughts take you to the early days of your next relationship, those days when you start feeling the buzz of falling in love again. It doesn't matter if all the people presently in your DM's are fvckboys or materialistic women, you only need 1 right person to show up. You know the type of person you wish to date, that and only that, should be your focus.

I'm not trying to put you on some empty motivational bullshit, but I really do want you to smile as you read this right now, feel the vibe of a new relationship, feel it in your bones. Do this for only 10 minutes, do it for 10 minutes today, do it for just 10 minutes everyday.

Dwelling on the past doesn't do anything for you than to steal your time and peace of mind.

You don't need to know how, where or when your next relationship is going to happen, just know that a greater love is coming to fill the void that this past relationship has created.

And please don't start over-think things to the point that when any guy says hello to you, you'll start thinking "Oh my, maybe this is him, maybe this is my Mr Right" Just take it nice and easy. You are allowed to feel an attraction towards anyone who happens to be your spec, but physical attraction it is, let it stay as just that. If the person intensifies their effort over the next couple weeks, then you can let go of your common sense small, just don't let your eagerness for a new relationship make you rush things.

Choose to control the thoughts your mind processes and don't let it run on freestyle mode. And why do I say this? Because hardly would your mind choose thoughts from a happy future that hasn't occurred yet, when it has real images from a past that just happened. Your mind has more files in its 'memory' department, than it has in the 'imagination' department, so it's going to require will-power from you, for your mind to focus strictly on its imagination department.

It's through your imagination that you'll start painting a picture of a better future for yourself, this is where thoughts that make you feel good are, and when you feel good, you make good decisions and you attract good things, getting one step closer to your idea of a meeting a better person

When we are heartbroken, we have the tendency to always be in a state of feeling regret, cheated, stupid or dejected- NO. Rather take valuable lessons from your memory and picture a similar situation like that re-occurring in the future, now visualize yourself meeting someone who treats you right, just the way you want, because from this day forward that's what you deserve and that's what you would attract! And if you were the one who did wrong, if you are the one who erred, now visualize yourself handling things more calmer and more maturely, understand that by picking the lesson out of this situation, you have automatically become a better person!

But what if I want to be single for a while?

That is totally valid, some people want to discover themself a bit more before they venture into another relationship, and I see a lot of sense in this. If being single is your motive, you still need to use your imaginations to assist yourself in healing from the hurt of a past relationship. Being single has its advantages, even though there might be times when you wish for the warmth of a partner, but then you are also spared of the emotional ups and downs of a relationship. The most beautiful part of being single is that you get learn more about yourself in that space and time.

CHAPTER 6

FINDING YOURSELF AGAIN

(Return of the mac)

Once my self-esteem is back to 100%
You'll be dead to me
- ***Anonymous***

Your Relationship Status: JBU

I am currently building a Dating Website as at the time of writing this book. It has been in the works for a while now. I plan to make it a a very social dating platform, but most importantly I need it to cater to the needs of introverts and people who don't like too much noise.

A lot of people want to mingle, but they want to do so in a calm respectable environment and not in a public-overcrowded manner. We now live a significant part of our social lives online, even a lot of ongoing relationships are developed over the phone (Video calls and chats) So I plan to include the wishes of quiet people in my social Dating platform.

One of the tech guys, developing the site suggested to me that we included JBU as one of the options of a person's relationship status.

JBU stands for *Just Broke Up*

I haven't agreed yet, as I am not sure if anyone would want to announce to the world that they *just broke up*, I think merely stating *'single'* does the job.

Now back to you, you are currently in that JBU status and you feel like you don't even know what you're going to do with yourself going forward. Everything you have done in the past months or years, you have done it with your ex, you have even drifted away from a lot of your close friends simply because you always planned your life around your relationship.

Now that you're single again, you feel like you no longer fit into any social circle.

It's very normal to be in this state after a break up, now you simply have to find yourself again. Some people like to use the phrase create yourself. I'm fine with both, find yourself, create yourself, as long as you are re-united with your true self again

You know deep down that you're more than this. You know what stuff you're made of, it's just falling-in-love that has softened you to this extent.

When a relationship crashes, it can steal a great deal of your self-esteem. You start to second guess your self-worth, you had viewed your world though the eyes of your ex, and when they gave up on you, you couldn't help but think that it had to do with your worth as a person.

But you're wrong! The fact that they walked away, or wanted something else doesn't have anything to do with your value as a person.

This is why you need to start trying to find yourself again, the earlier you do this, the earlier you're able to start healing.

Now there's no rush here, healing happens one day at a time.

You won't even have answers to a lot of questions bothering you right now, but here's the thing, the answers do not need to exist today, the answers would come to you as you grow through this phase, one step at a time.

We all don't know what exactly to do with ourselves after a hurtful break up, so you are not alone.

I know a lot of people who, after breaking up, they started thinking all day all night, losing weight, being drained, but as they grew past that phase, they look back and start laughing at themself wondering "How could I have been that desperate"

I know people who begged and begged their ex, did ridiculous things like kneeling down in the middle of the highway, jumping a 15-foot fence, only to look back and realize that they just let over-thinking get the best of them.

Trust me, your mind is blowing a lot of things out of proportion right now.

It's really important that after a break up, you spend time with yourself, so you can rediscover your strengths and weaknesses.

It sounds basic, but it is so damn important.

Finding yourself gives you something to work with in future relationships, you have a more accurate idea of what your limits are. You get to know deep down in your heart what you can tolerate and what you will not tolerate.

In this social media era, there are a lot of opinions flying left and right on how relationships should be. So much unsolicited advice would come your way, this is why it's very important that you have your own moral center. You'll know what feels good to you deep down and what doesn't, so you don't go into the next relationship just because friends are hyping you.

You are just coming out of a journey where you gave a significant part of yourself to another person, his or her absence is definitely going to create a vacuum, oh yes it will and that vacuum cannot be filled in a day, it takes time.

Some people are tempted to use the presence of a new lover to pass through this phase, but this has it's risks. Your sense on judgement might be clouded by the fact that you are scared of being alone, so you might jump into the relationship just to avoid loneliness. Although the dating world doesn't operate with the law of mathematics, in the game of love and emotions nothing is predictable, so I'm not saying it is a crime to fall in love with a new person immediately after you break up. I have seen people get out of a relationship and hurry into another one and their new relationship became a great relationship that ended up on the alter.

All I'm saying is- don't rush the process. *Good things come to those who wait*, I would rather you spend some time with yourself and solidify your self-esteem back to where it should be, so even if you start liking someone, you wouldn't be easily blinded. You would be able to smell bullshit from a mile away.

When you take time to find yourself, having a relationship would only be another reason for you to be happy. You have already found your happy by yourself, a partner just adds extra flavor to your 'happy'. That way you wouldn't define your whole existence through the way you're treated in a relationship.

Of course, you should still love with all your heart. Oh yes! You should give yourself a chance to fall deeply in love. Half-loving doesn't fulfil you, so you want to love and you want to love fully. Love, just like life, is a risk and if you want to get any juice out of it, you have to be willing to take risks.

But I'll repeat it again, finding yourself makes your common-sense stay on, so in case the person you start falling for happens to be a wolf in sheep's clothing, you would detect it early on, and bounce before it becomes stories that touch. This doesn't mean it wouldn't hurt, even if it's just 1 month you spend with a person, it still hurts when they turn out to just be another phony lover. It can be emotionally exhausting.

So how do I find myself again?

When our sense of self-worth takes a dip, we tend to compromise a little too much on the way we let people treat us. It doesn't even have to be a romantic relationship, even with our friends, we bend and condone more shit than we should. So you need to replace that self talk in your head that makes you feel less. Work at it every day, even if you have to stand in front of the mirror, look deep into your reflection's eyes and say some powerful **I AM** affirmations e.g. I am beautiful, I am worthy, I am blessed etc.

If you are Nigerian then you'll be familiar with these funny affirmations that trended online a while ago. It was funny, but powerful (I'm actually laughing right now)

The affirmations went like this:

I am beauty

I am a spec

I drip glory

I am nobody's ex.

Haters will hate

Potatoes will potate

But my blood, shall never dry.

We move!!!

The first step to finding yourself again, is to deflect that voice in your head that's draining your confidence, as that is not the voice of the real you, the real you is actually the one listening to that voice that's talking crap, so tell it in a louder voice to shut up!

Secondly, do not underestimate the power of leaning on friends at this time. Spending time alone can be hard at this point, because the voices in our head that make us over-think are very bold when we are alone.

Don't let your mind convince you to stay back at home when your friends are stepping out for a movie or something. I'm not saying you should start partying all night and getting high every other day, but stepping out of the house in some manner really does help. You don't even have to mingle with people of the opposite sex, just go for events, and see other humans laughing and having fun, even if you sit in a corner thinking of your ex, please just step out of the house.

You are in a battle with your senses, so I need you to drown that demoralizing self talk that emerged from the way you were treated in your past relationship, that is not you, you are worth more than that.

I know when you go into another relationship, you would want your new partner to give you their all, just as you would want to feel secure enough to love him/her without being cautious and that's great, **but you cannot give what you don't own.** How can you give yourself to another, when even you yourself do not own yourself? So taking it easy with yourself during this period of re-finding you is very important to your future relationship.

CHAPTER 7

SHOULD WE STAY FRIENDS?

(Who friend epp?)

Your ex asking you
to be friends after a break up
is like kidnappers asking you
to keep in touch after letting you go
- ***Anonymous***

Should you stay friends? - My answer is first NO, then maybe YES but that 'YES' has to be later on. If you are hurting, then I don't think you should be friends. At least not for now.

Please, please, please do not sabotage your healing process by lying to yourself that it's a harmless friendship.

You might be saying:

"I've already accepted that it's over between us, but we have been so used to each other all this while so we can't stop being close just like that"

Stop lying to yourself!

You don't even want to be 'just friends' with this person, you have been more than friends with him/her before, and you still wish it was so. What you really want is to continue being their lover, their boo, their everyday ride or die, but that is not happening any longer.

You're hanging around, selling yourself cheaper every day, hoping that maybe by some chance they would change their mind and decide to get back with you and every day that you hang around that vibe, getting less than you really wish to get, you are killing your sense of self-worth and drowning your emotional self the more.

A part of you would be living in constant fear wondering if they have started seeing someone new. I know because I have been there, done that. It's not worth it.

Not been friends with a person, doesn't mean you are enemies, it just means you are not friends- simple!

It is easy for us to go from friends to lovers, but it is an uphill task, trying to re-adjust from lovers to friends (when the hurt of the break-up is still very fresh).

It's very easy for the person who is less hurt in the break-up to suggest that you should remain friends and continue seeing each other once in a while. Men do this a lot, especially when he's still enjoying occasional sex between you two. Women also do it, when they know that the guy they're breaking up with is a good guy and for some reason she still wants to have him under her control, or maybe there's some type of benefit she's still getting from having him around. She then blows hot and cold, telling him on one hand that they're done, while on the other hand still letting him feel like he should be protecting her.

Being in this situation with your ex, and still having sex with them might satisfy your heart briefly, but it hurts your soul in the long run. Don't do it, you'll become a shadow of yourself, second guessing your worth every step of the way.

CUT IT OFF!!!

You don't need that vibe right now, you're not fighting, you're protecting your mental. Eventually you would heal to a point where you're not even bothered by your ex's vibe anymore, then you can establish communication again if you want. At that point, you'll no longer define your existence through the validation you get from him/her, and that is the 'healing' that we're discussing all through this book.

What if my ex is pushing for friendship and he/she seems sincere about it?

No one said you guys should turn to enemies. Like I said earlier, because we don't talk often doesn't mean we're now enemies.

If your ex is pushing for friendship, you too push for space-ship.

Don't forget that people would empower the agenda that favors them. Some people would use your presence to make their own moving on process easier. On one hand they want to leave you, on the other hand they want to be able to monitor your progress, and make sure you don't bounce back so fast that they now start to hurt from how well and how quickly you healed.

It was after a few broken relationships, that I learnt the hard-way and realized that in life YOU HAVE TO BE INTENTIONAL ABOUT YOUR HEALING.

Your ex, who put you in this situation cannot be the same person that would get you out of it. Each time you try to move on, it would be like taking one step forward and two steps backward as his/her presence would keep re-igniting the very memories you are trying to get rid of.

No one can walk that journey for you, you've got to do it yourself. Your friends, your siblings can be there for you, understanding and all, but you are the only one who would dictate how you grow through it.

So save the friendship and niceties for later when you have gotten a grip of your emotional state, for now I urge you to please PROTECT YOURSELF, PROTECT YOUR VIBE, AT ALL COST.

CHAPTER 8

SHOULD I CALL?

(I really need to get closure)

The healthiest type of closure
Is the one 'time' gives to you
- Atewo Laolu-Ogunniyi

It's very normal that you miss your ex so much some days that you think you'll go crazy.

And it's also okay if one day you picked the phone and called him/her and tried to talk about what you both shared, maybe they didn't even pick and you dropped a dozen missed calls and sent one long-ass message, pouring out all your heart and feelings.

It's all part of the 'moving on' phase. You're not expected to become some cold-hearted person overnight, nope! Moving on from somebody you cared so much about, doesn't happen just like that.

Some days you would break down and feel betrayed, some days you'll be angry, some days you would blame yourself unnecessarily.

What I would not allow you to do, is remain in that low state of mind. I know the beauty that awaits you in your future, on your behalf I can feel the goodness that's coming on way already. Amen?

But now you're struggling with an aching desire to pick up the phone and dial your ex's number.

Listen to me, there is nothing you're calling to say. Haven't you noticed that the few times when you called and spoke your mind, you ended up being more confused after the call? Nothing tangible was said and the questions still continued popping up in your head.

I'M NOT JOKING, I REALLY NEED THIS CLOSURE

Closure does not come from without, it comes from within. You won't get closure by talking to your ex, you'll get closure by talking to yourself.

True closure is less about you getting clarity of why you guys broke-up and more about you accepting the fact that the break-up has happened and now you should be prioritizing your healing.

It is our refusal to accept reality that causes most conflict in our mental.

If you call ex or go to see him/her, there is no guarantee that you would see logical sense in their reason for breaking up with you. You both can sit down and have an 8 hour conversation and you would still be weighed down afterwards.

The feeling of 'I need closure' is just our emotions trying to get short term satisfaction and the thing about feeding your emotions is that the more you feed it, the hungrier it gets.

Even if you get some closure now, you would probably be triggered by a statement that your ex made during the conversation, so you'll be needing another episode of closure for that statement, then after that you'll still need closure for other questions in your head, and so it goes on and on for weeks, months and the emotional draining continues instead of your healing.

WHAT IF MY EX CALLS, ASKING FOR US TO SEE?

Act one, Scene one

Lady: My ex called today, he said it's been a while, that he'd like us to see each other and talk

Best Friend: What are you guys talking about again, you don't need to see him, he has nothing to offer you anymore, abeg he has broken your heart enough. Just let him be.

Lady: I know but, let me just hear what he has to say this time.

Best Friend: This is the 100th time you're hearing what he has to say, you guys would only end up having sex, without discussing anything tangible.

Lady: Sex? Never! I already told you I'm never having sex with him again, ever! I've passed that staged nau. I'm not even going to stay long at all.

Best friend shrugs in disbelief.

Lady then uses her own hard-earned money to get an uber and head to ex boyfriend's place. She settles in after he gave her a tight-warm hug at the door.

It has been a while she has been to his house, nothing much has changed. She heads to the refrigerator and laughs as he tells her he made sure to have her favorite drink in there.

They talk about life in general, crack some old jokes and he puts on a TV series, they're not really watching, so the TV just blabs in the background...

A few moments later

Kpakiti! Kpakiti! Kpakiti

Chookwudi! Chookwudi! Chookwudi!

Sex sounds all over the house!

She promised herself she would not sleep with him, but somehow someway she has landed on the D.

She goes home and realizes they actually didn’t talk about anything worthwhile, all they did was knack!

End of scene

*****

It wouldn’t have been so bad if she had already gotten over him, then it would have just been a case of *‘sex-with-the-ex’*, but she hasn't gotten over him yet, and the sex has only made things worse, fading emotions have been re-ignited. That quick satisfaction of seeing him and spending time with him has set her moving on process back a couple of weeks or even months.

So when he called and said they should see, she should have calmly declined. It might have been hard in the moment, but she would be stronger for it, and she would have healed a vital part of her mental.

Let your brain do the thinking for you and not your emotions. Your future self would thank you for that!

CHAPTER 9

SHOULD I SEND A BIRTHDAY GIFT

(You're kidding right?)

Sometimes you have to forget what you feel and remember what you deserve

- Anonymous

This is was not even supposed to be a chapter on its own, but because I know you have coconut head I had to make it one so I can hammer this point into your head well well.

I know you'll keep looking for any tiny reason to reach out to your ex, anything to just establish contact and what better excuse do you have than his/her birthday that's coming up.

You might even start thinking of a gift to send, racking your brain for the perfect present to get. But is it really needed? Do you have to?

If you were already in a new relationship where you are so madly on love with your new lover, would you be buying your ex a birthday gift? Would you even call to wish him/her 'happy birthday'? I'm pretty sure you wouldn't, because you would be enjoying every moment of your new life with the new person.

So even if you don't have a new lover yet, you're still in a relationship. In-fact you're constantly in the most important relationship of your life and that relationship is the one you have with yourself. You need to start respecting and loving yourself just like you would do to someone you are madly in love with. You have to start placing value on you, and stop making decisions that put you in second place.

I know a lady who heard that her ex fell sick. She quickly called his phone to check up on him. *"Are you okay now? How do you feel? Make sure you use your drugs" I'll check up on you tomorrow"*

Jesus! This dude only had malaria for 3 days, and here you are forming extra care. Like I said, if you are in a new relationship would you be doing all the excessive nonsense? I bet you wouldn't. Now see what the next chapter says.

CHAPTER 10

WE MOVE!!!

(Don't Hate, But Don't Care)

I don't have 'ex's,
I have Y's.
As in Y the hell did I do that?
- ***Anonymous***

Don't hate, don't!

Don't go nurturing feelings of hatred for your ex.

Don't even think of getting revenge. There's a saying that goes *"Revenge is like slapping yourself, expecting the other person to feel the pain".*

Negative feelings affect us more than it affects the person that we are feeling negative towards. To be able to hate someone, you would need to give 'hatred' a home to stay, and that home is your heart, since it is 'your hate', This is why I strongly advice against hating your ex.

The sole intention of negative feelings is to make your world revolve around the thing you hate and its entry point into your mind, is through your ego and your vanity, the lower versions of you. Emotions that spur from hatred distract you from moving on to the better things that lay ahead for you.

If your ex betrayed and hurt you so badly when you guys broke up, find the strength to forgive him/her.

FORGIVE- The word itself is made up of 2 syllables *Fore* and *Give.* It simply means you GIVE the offender your positivity, your peace, beFORE they prove they are deserving of it, or even before they apologize for the wrong they did to you. When you forgive someone, you have protected your light and your higher vibes more than you can ever imagine.

Your heart might be aching, your mind might be arguing with you, but your soul is refreshed and more in tune with goodness of the universe.

Now because you have forgiven someone, doesn't mean you need to have them in your life. Even the Bible urges us to forgive, but it doesn't tell us to forget.

For example, the lady I spoke about in the previous chapter (who was calling up her ex when she heard that he was sick) didn't need to call and start fussing over him. She could easily have wished him well in her heart and continue with her life.

Oprah Winfrey once said *"You can love someone and still choose to say goodbye to them, you can miss a person every day and still be glad that they're no longer in your life"*

This is what I call moving on gracefully. People try to make it seem like once you don't care about a person, that equates to you hating them, and nothing could be further from the truth.

If you have read the book 'The Subtle Art Of Not Giving A fuck by Mark Manson, he explains that we all have a limited number of fucks to give in our lifetime. Inevitably, you have to give a fuck about something in life, but if you want to be happy and successful, you simply have to make sure that you're giving a fuck about the right things.

As far as this book you're reading is concerned- YOU DON'T NEED TO GIVE A FUCK ABOUT YOUR EX!

No hate, no negative vibes, just zero fucks given.

There's a tendency to want to use hate to push out the residual feelings of love you might still be feeling for your ex, but that's not healthy in the long run. You might start rebelling against the whole idea of love and that blocks you from the possibilities of sweet loving out there. Too much hate for your ex can even have you hating on the opposite sex so much that it affects your next relationship, as you would be analyzing your new lover through the aura of your ex, and that's not right, as you need to give each person a chance to prove themself.

How a lack of confidence can have us caring about our ex.

Sometimes we define our worth as a human being through the way we love our partner, and when that partner walks out of our life and we don't yet have another person to give all that love to, we simply try to continue giving it to them, even if they are not receptive or reciprocating it.

We feel less of a human being when we don't have someone to love and to be loved in return. We feel we're not desirable to anyone. This is a lie that the insecure part of our mind tries to sell to us. You will love and be loved again!

This is why you need to prioritize your relationship with yourself, you are worth it and for now all your love should be given to you by you.

Don't listen to that small inner voice that attempts to make you feel stupid, don't pay attention to friends who try to make you feel like you have been played. You haven't been played, you haven't been a fool and you haven't been stupid. Even if it happened that your ex hurt you multiple times before the relationship crashed, you have just done your part, you made your sacrifices and invested in something you believed in, but sadly it didn't work out the way you wanted.

Of course, you are wiser now, and you would better be able to spot red flags from afar, so if a new person comes around in the future and you see familiar negative behaviors in them, you would take a step back quick before you get emotionally entwined in an ugly situation again.

CHAPTER 11

OUT OF SIGHT IS OUT OF MIND

(Physical and mental distance)

I maintain my sanity
by keeping my distance
- Luis Miguel

When a person is addicted to masturbation and wishes to quit, they are advised to stop watching porn immediately. The person is also advised to look away from anything that can trigger sexual thoughts their mind, it might just be a mild erotic video or a seemingly harmless conversation with friends where they're painting sexual pictures with their words.

These things are called triggers, and avoiding them is the first step a masturbator should take to win the mental battle against the addiction.

Different strategies work for different people who successfully overcome an addiction, but the common denominator among all of them is that they avoid the triggers.

So what are **the triggers** that make you want to see your ex, what are the things that can direct your thoughts to your ex, even if you weren't thinking of him/her before?

1. Keeping many pictures of your ex on your phone is definitely a major trigger. We spend a reasonable amount of time on our phones these days, and a quick journey to your photo gallery would send you down memory lane.

2. If your friends keep bringing up unnecessary conversation about your ex to you e.g. they go to an event and they spotted him/her there, so they come back and they're giving you all the details. Of course, you won't tell your friends not to tell you what they saw, because you yourself are dying to hear the gist. "What was she wearing, did she look good?" Was he alone or he came with someone?" "He came in a new car, which type?"

3. If you keep hanging out at the same spot where you know your ex is always frequenting, then there is a high chance you would run into each other. As a matter of fact, once you're at the spot, you wouldn't be relaxed, you would keep looking over your shoulder at everyone who walks in, not knowing how to act when you finally see him/her.

To be able to move on, you need to set up physical distance between you and your ex. Don't go to that spot where you know it's possible to see them, you don't want to end up having a messed-up evening. Don't go to his/her house all in the name of 'we just want to talk'... it hardly ends as just talk

Create mental distance by letting your friends know it's over between you and your ex, so they should reduce the feedback they bring to you when they see him/her outside. The less you hear the better. There's really nothing you want to do with such unnecessary information, your moving on process does not need it.

I remember one time when I was hurting from one of my 'breakfast servings' and I was still trying to heal. I was in my brother's car, he was driving and I had slept off in the front passenger's seat. We literally drove passed my ex in traffic, she was in the front seat of an SUV and a guy was driving. She saw my brother and waved, he waved back and just continued driving, I was asleep and he didn't even wake me up. Not only didn't he wake me up, he didn't even mention it to me for months. It was long after I had moved on that he told me of that incident.

Now that was a great move he did right there. On the day it happened I would have wanted him to wake me up in that car, or at least tell me about it when we got home. But looking back at it, was it not better that I didn't see that image that day? It would not have helped my 'moving on process' to see her in another man's car? I would have gone into over-thinking mode straight.

If you have pictures of your ex on your phone, you either delete them, or copy them to a computer or flash drive where you don't have easy access to them. You don't want to be out, having a good day and start looking for something on your phone only to stumble across a picture of 2 of you smiling together-That alone can make you forget why you brought out your phone in the first place.

If you both were a couple who took a lot of goofy pictures, then you should be deleting about 90% of those pictures. Those are past memories now, and you need to let the past stay where it belongs- in the past. There might be some memories that you don't want to get rid of, then store them away somewhere. But when you get into a new relationship, you might want to re-consider this, as you don't want your new partner to discover a hidden folder on your laptop full of pictures of you and your ex. It's pointless.

The few things I suggested here might not be so easy because a part of you wants to hold on to some memories, but it is the best thing you can do for yourself and to make your healing process more bearable.

CHAPTER 12

BUT I SEE MY EX ALL THE TIME

(Co-parenting, Work at same office)

One of the happiest moments in life
is when you find the courage
to let go of what you can't change.
- ***Anonymous***

Co-parenting

Co-parenting is such a deep topic to discuss with many different angles, but the scope of this book would not be covering all the angles. Here we would be focusing on *'How to get over an ex that you are co-parenting with'.*

When you have a child with someone, you are basically bound together for life. The hard thing is when you and this person no longer continue as lovers, but you still have feelings for them. That's a pretty tough position to be in.

In the game of 'moving on', proximity plays a great role in your healing process. Just as we discussed in the last chapter- *maintain physical distance.* Now this is hard to achieve when you are raising a child together as the well-being of the child requires that you interact with your ex often and as peacefully as possible.

So how do I go about it?

1. First of all, you have to face the reality of the situation as quickly as your heart can permit, this would guide you on what new boundaries must come into place when you communicate with your ex. You do not

have the luxury of living in denial like people who don't have a child together.

Conversations between both of you should be limited to the welfare of your child, don't try to capitalize on the fact that both of you have to talk often and start using that chance to ask personal questions. You are not entitled to know most of their personal details any longer, same way he/she is not eligible to know yours too. The only details you need to know now, are the ones that have to do with the well-being of your child.

2. Don't use your child as a reason to get closer than required. The break-up has happened, if the your ex has lost interest in the idea of 'both-of-you', then they'll probably know when you're trying to use the child to have your way and this would only repel them the more. This is why I said you do not have the luxury of living in denial, because you would get so consumed by your desire to be with this person, that you won't see how much you're using the child to try and push your own agenda.

3. Earlier on in this book, I said Don't *Hate, But Don't Care,* well this applies to you in a little different manner because you have to care about your ex in the capacity of the fact that he/she is also your child's

parent. This doesn't mean that you need to care all the way, but in the interest of your child, you would need to keep up to date with your ex, so when the child asks 'How is Daddy or How is Mummy', you would have a ready answer. All these can be done within the new boundaries set.

I already said this book cannot cover the whole scope of co-parenting, that's not the aim of this piece of work. This book is concerned with 'getting over your ex' so the couple I am addressing here, are definitely the ones that are both active in the child's life.

4. Do not use your child as a weapon against your ex. There's a thin line between love and hate, so if your ex appears to be moving on faster than you, maybe they're now seeing someone else, do not get so upset that you start using the child for petty fights. Not only would you be hurting the child in the process (which is terrible) you would also be hindering yourself from moving on.

5. Life does not end with this person. If you're a woman and you're thinking people might not want to marry you because you already have a child, I'm here to tell you that is a myth. A real man wants a woman who would give him peace of mind, if he sees that in you,

he would take your child as his own, people wouldn't even know he is not the biological father. I see single mother's finding love everytime. Some of the stories are so beautiful you would think it was scripted.

So the most important thing when trying to get over the feelings you still have for your *baby-daddy* or *baby-mama* is to set boundaries and don't cross them. This is your best shot at protecting your sanity. You already know they don't want to continue dating you, so put a leash on your desire to always want to elongate a conversation, don't do it.

Some exes know you still have feelings for them, so they start telling you how their plans are going and all, knowing very well that your curiosity would be steered. In a scenario like this, keep the conversation leveled, don't ask questions that would make him/her talk more, as a matter of fact, circle the conversation back to issues concerning your child. If you don't do this they would continue teasing you for as long as you allow, enjoying the power of attraction they still have over you. So stay aware and guard your mental space.

This last point is totally up to you, your self control has to be applied here. If you feel that he or she wants to come back to you, you can play along and see where the vibe heads to, but if you come to realize that it's just a situation where they're blowing hot today and blowing cold tomorrow, meanwhile they're steady moving on, then please don't hang around for such low-level treatment. When you place a value on yourself, then your ex would value you.

WORK AT SAME OFFICE

For the younger audience reading this book, you can read the headline above as 'Studying at same school'

This falls under the predicament of not being able to establish physical distance from the person you're trying to get over. That makes all the difference in your case, as you are constantly reminded of their existence. I am not going to sugarcoat it, you are in a tougher situation than people who have some distance from their ex.

I know a lady who spends an extra 10 minutes at the car park before she enters the office, because she knows it's another day where she would be seeing her ex all around the workplace, acting like he wasn't affected by the break up.

An office is an enclosed community and the social life in that space is different from the outside world. If your colleagues don't know you dated this person, then that's one less thing to worry about for you. Keep it that way and don't let the hurt of the situation make you start talking around the office.

But if your colleagues know you dated this person, you would feel their questioning eyes boring into your skin whenever something involving that person happens, meanwhile you would be trying to put up an act like you're not as bothered as you actually are.

So, here's what you can do

1. **Change your office routine after an office break up**. Your unpredictability would make people back off from teasing or asking unnecessary questions. No doubt it's a tough position, but it's not an impossible one. Switch things up, this would give you a path to clearer thinking in that small space.

   It could be changing your sitting position, if your office allows that.

   You can change the time you leave from work at the close of business.

   You can change the time you go for your break so you would have less chances of bumping into your ex.

2. **Don't confide in your colleagues,** except that person is a very close friend of yours, who you're certain is not going to turn your story into the next hot gossip at break time. Do not be tempted to air out your grievances to just anyone, simply because they are willing to listen. Some people just want to be entertained by your reality. Stick to your trusted friends or confide in someone who doesn't work in your office environment.

3. **Let your work distract you.** Before, it was your office relationship that was distracting you from your work, but right now you need to let your work distract you from the just-ended-office relationship. When going through a break up, people need some form of distraction to power through, like going out with friends, finding a new hobby or even changing environment. In this case, since you're pretty much stuck in the same environment with this person, then use your work as distraction during those office hours.

As the days goes by, you would heal more and more and it would become easier to handle.

CHAPTER 13

STRENGTH OR WEAKNESS

(Your choice)

You never know how strong you are,
until being strong is your only choice
- ***Bob Marley***

We are gradually getting to the end of this book, and I just want to use this last chapters to reiterate some of the most important things we have discussed.

In the preceding pages, you have learnt a lot on 'how to get over your ex', but is knowing enough?

People know what to do, but most people don't do what they know. Would you be able to apply all that you have read here? It's easier read than done.

The situation has thrown itself at you and it's not a pleasant one.

Now what version of yourself are you going to throw back at the situation? The weak version of you, or the strong version?

Weakness offers us nothing productive.

I know you are strong enough to pull through this, and not only pull through, you would even become a better person in the process.

Every single day you hold yourself back from unnecessarily stalking or trying to know what your ex is up to, you are getting a bit of yourself back, you are getting stronger. It is a constant tussle between the higher you and the lower you.

Do not let your mind play tricks on you, do not allow yourself to be bothered with panic thoughts of whether he/she has met someone else. Do not measure the rate at which your ex is moving on, you are not the same, yes you shared something together, but you are two different people, your 'moving on' pattern is so not going to be the same.

Do not grant yourself the short-term satisfaction of seeing what your ex is up to, stalking them but ending up causing yourself more psychological pain in the long run.

You get to choose how this moving-on stage goes. The choices you make would define if you'll **GO** through this or if you'll **GROW** through it. Go through it and it would linger somewhere in your reality in the future, but grow through it and you would look back at this times and laugh real hard. You would see your ex and you wouldn't even feel a pinch.

Keep this quote in mind- *Life is lived forward, but understood backwards.*

Many times, we go through a situation, it seems like the world has come to an end, but looking back much later, we start wondering why we almost killed ourself.

You got this, keep your head up!

CHAPTER 14

CHOOSE YOUR MOODS

(Take It One Day At a Time)

Just keep moving forward
one day at a time.
The view from the top is so worth the climb
- ***Anonymous***

When you break up with a person, a part of you at that moment goes with the relationship. That is why we feel empty immediately after a break up.

Now this missing part of you would grow back, it always does and it doesn't have to be until you get into another relationship before you feel complete. You will **'grow'** back to being one with yourself again.

But growth just like every other thing that nature controls, can only be done one day at a time, you have to endure/enjoy the process. At the end of the day, you would be more than glad to meet the person you have become when this growth in your life is completed.

You can't rush your growth, your healing any more than you can rush next summer to come quicker, it can only come one day at a time.

What you can do however, is to make every day of the growing process easier for yourself, you can make each day more bearable.

Yes- you very much have that within your power, and since it comes at you only one day at a time, the better for you, because one day isn't be impossible to handle.

How can I make each day more bearable? How can I make this pain go away?

Choose your moods!

Choose your freaking moods!!

It sounds like something you don't have control over, right? Well, you do have control, you have more control over your moods than you have been made to believe.

Before, you used to deal with your moods subconsciously, but now, during this 'growing back' phase, you need to be more conscious of a lot of things you allow to enter your head and run your mind. Some of the things that affect our moods are social media, conversations with friends, music and movies. It's time for you to pay closer attention to the type of content you consume and the talks you participate in.

If you get carried away in gossip and hang around your friends when they are talking about how there is no guy/girl out there to date again, no marriage material out there, you might start thinking you have lost your one shot at having a happy life. But don't forget, peoples gist and opinions are only limited to what they are going through at that point in time. Walk away when you see that the topic of discussion is beginning to make you think. There's no heroic move by staying and soaking yourself in heartache.

What pages are you following on social media? A lot of pages are set up just to maximize traffic, so most of their posts are alarming posts that can scare the shit out of you. The people who run these pages know that humans are more attracted to alarming news so that's what they post. Don't follow these pages, they'll cloud up your mind and view of relationships more than you can ever imagine.

Music, is also another thing that highly affects our moods. *Music is spiritual.* Music is the only profession that exists in heaven and earth at the same time. After all we don't have doctors, engineers or lawyers in heaven, but we have choirs and music. Music can lift or dampen your mood in minutes.

Right now, your spirit has been let down, please don't feed it with food that would keep it down, don't.

It's not going to do you any good to be wallowing in self-pity, or to cuddle up in bed listening to songs that talk about lost lovers and broken hearts. *Stay away from heartbreak songs for now, put on some lively music, inhale, exhale and live in the moment.*

Right now you might be thinking, *"what's Peeshaun suggesting, this is not realistic, this would just be a case of me lying to myself".* Don't worry about facing reality at this point, reality has already faced you, and you are really getting a heavy dose of it, for you to have read this book up to this point, you really want to learn new things, so allow yourself to do just that.

Your Ex was your old reality, you need to invite and welcome a new reality.

It wouldn't happen in a day as I mentioned earlier, but do yourself the huge favour of making the transition period easier, you owe yourself that much, you really do. Change your music playlist to upbeat songs, distract the pain for a day, distract it for 3 days, do it for 5 days, 7 days and you have pretty much gone a week without dying so much inside.

Don't even judge yourself if you are finding it hard, to get over him/her, you probably loved hard and loving hard is a good thing (when it's with the right person).

So if the tears come, allow yourself to cry, don't hold it back, roll on the bed if you like, stay indoors for the day if you like, no problem. When you are done, go back to choosing your moods again and try to continue deflecting the sad feelings one at a time.

CHAPTER 15

BACK TO THE FUTURE

(Amazing times ahead)

Every positive thought
is an investment
in your future
- ***Anonymous***

If you are actually going through a heartbreak right now, I wish could let you see, how certain the future is, how certain it is that you would fall in love with someone better and more compatible with you.

When in pain, we get lost in the moment, thinking this is all there is to life, but that's a lie. It's our minds way of playing hide and seek with us.

Your mind shows you pictures of all the good times you had with your ex, teasing you about all the things you might be missing now that you have broken up. But that's our weakness as imperfect humans. Without realizing it, you start living in the past mentally. You aren't missing what you had with your ex, you are missing what you wish you had. It's not like the relationship was a perfect one. In a few years you might see that it was a blessing that it all ended.

What if that relationship was a trap, and the break up is God yanking you away from it? What if it's just not God's masterplan for you?

Never be afraid to trust an unknown future to a known God

Your next relationship would be epic!

NOTE: If you keep looking for your ideal relationship in the past, you might miss it when it comes in the future. Face front, there's goodness ahead!

On a final note, just because someone doesn't want you is less about you and more about them. It doesn't mean you aren't good enough, trust me there is a better person out there searching for you and all you have to offer. Don't beat yourself up over this and even if you did make some mistakes, don't blame yourself more than you deserve. Now you know better, now you have learnt, take these lessons and forge ahead, there's a new dawn looming for you over the horizon.

The End.

www.ingramcontent.com/pod-product-compliance
Ingram Content Group UK Ltd.
Pitfield, Milton Keynes, MK11 3LW, UK
UKHW040031200726
13854UKWH00001B/469